DR. JOHN POLIS

PATTERN FOR GLORY

LIVING IN THE MANIFEST PRESENCE OF GOD

FOREWORD BY DR. RON COTTLE

PATTERN FOR GLORY
Living In The Manifest Presence Of God
By Dr. John Polis

PAPERBACK ISBN: 978-1-7377236-8-4
Also available in Hardback and eBook versions

Prepared for Publication By

MAKING YOUR BOOK A REALITY
Cedar Point, NC | 843-929-8768 | info@BandBpublishingLLC.com

Original Transcription Editing By

Susans.Servant.Services@gmail.com

To Contact the Author
JOHN POLIS MINISTRIES
PO BOX 1007 | Beaufort, SC 29901
drjohn@rfiusa.org | www.rfiusa.org

CONTENTS

Endorsements

Dr. John makes a passionate and extensive presentation concerning the times and seasons that we are currently in. Like the sons of Issachar who had understanding of the times and knew what Israel should do, likewise, Dr. John prophetically understands the times we are in, but also through apostolic wisdom and grace he reveals how to appropriate it within the body of Christ as mature sons. The world will never know the glory until the church encounters the glory, and then the church has the responsibility to manifest the glory. We are called to be glory carriers. When the pattern is right, the glory will fall. Glory doesn't show up accidentally. What is the glory? It's the manifestation of Christ clearly seen. And the time has come for the sons of God to manifest the glory of God as it has been so eloquently written in the pages of this book. There are a few authorities in the apostolic movement who could offer such insight, foresight, and balanced perspective of the times and seasons that we are in like Dr. John. This masterpiece "The Glorious Church" is a spiritual GPS to lead the church of Jesus Christ into the age of glory! This is a must read, read it and read it again!

Royal Regards,
Dr. Mark Kauffman
Website: drmarkkauffman.org

Dr. John Polis has gifted the body of Christ tools of knowledge for 'Living in the Presence of God.' The brilliant details written within this book map the path and the pattern for the ekklesia to obtain and live in the manifested glory. This book reveals a plethora of wisdom and revelation that can only be obtained through experience and intense study. Pattern for Glory is a book I highly recommend and will utilize in my ministry.

Pastor Josh Morgan
Covenant Church
Fairmont, WV

In pure Dr. John Polis fashion this is a pastor's handbook for building a strong and healthy last days church. It is scripturally based and easy to read, understand, and put into action.

I am privileged to have Dr. John Polis as my spiritual father since 1986. I have walked through the steps laid out in these pages and know they work. If you will apply the information from years of prayer, and study, shared within these pages, you will be spared much church hurt and disappointment for yourself and others you lead. His gift to articulate truths and biblical mysteries surrounding the Apostolic Parenting truths has taken both myself, and my husband from orphans to sons, and now we are spiritual parents with many sons and daughters across the map. I have seen "Pattern For Glory" work in the church as a spiritual daughter for over 38 years.

We were sent out to follow the pattern, and founded a church in another city and have grown to having our own apostolic network of pastors, churches, missions, shortwave radio, TV programs, and bible colleges. The proof of this biblical pattern laid out from cover to cover will work, because it truly is the "Pattern For Glory".

There are numerous sermons contained in each chapter that can easily be preached. As you will see Dr. John Polis is a teacher of teachers, and a preacher of preachers, as well as a world renown Apostle for the day in which we live, with the ability to share these timely truths and principles infused with hard-won wisdom.

Dr. Rena Perozich
MFC Ministries, Inc.
drrenaperozich.com

Foreword

DR. RON COTTLE

Here is another strong, practical, stirring book from one of God's genuine warrior Apostles, Dr. John Polis. As always, it is hard-hitting and to the point! This marine -- once one, always one -- doesn't do it any other way except wide open.

Prepare to be blessed by keen insight into the Word and the heart of God as you read. You'll get lots of quotable, memorable nuggets along the way. But read it all -- it's a strong word that marks out a pattern of growth and maturity leading to God's glorious church on earth, an expression of the Kingdom of God in your sphere of life and responsibility.

John has "been there and done that" in his long experience in ministry. His long tenure in Fairmont, West Virginia, where he has been an evangelist, shepherd, teacher, prophet and now apostolic father qualifies him to write such a book from his storehouse of understanding and experience. Read it and re-read it, for John has lived the pattern he describes so passionately here. He is his own "proof of the pudding".

I recommend this book to every believer in Christ at whatever stage or level of spiritual maturity you have reached. It is informative and instructive for growing, developing leaders in the Body who are seeking their own unique pattern for building the glorious church in their sphere; it is affirming for those who have found a working pattern and are walking it out with all the ups and downs, joys and heartaches associated with that; and it is reassuring for those who, like John himself, have been there and done that, and are now sharing their experiences and wisdom with spiritual sons and daughters coming along behind in this new, exciting generation.

Thanks, John! This book will be a great tool of ministry and inspiration for life leaders everywhere, both inside and outside the local church, whether in business or any of the professions.

Ronald E. Cottle, Ph.D., Ed.D.
Founder and President, Embassy College

Pictured above Dr. Ron Cottle (left) and Dr. John Polis (right).

Chapter One

ACCORDING TO PATTERN

I think we could all agree, that we want a great outpouring of the manifest presence of God in our personal lives and churches. However, a sustained outpouring of His glory does not happen by accident, it happens when we line ourselves up with God's pattern, doing things God's way. If you want to have an open Heaven then this book is for you. To get us started, let us look at Exodus 39,

> *"The Israelites had done all the work just as the Lord had commanded Moses. Moses inspected the work and saw that they had done it just as the Lord had commanded.*

So, Moses blessed them." Exodus 39:42-43 NIV

One of the first things we can see is that the presence of God that manifests in the Glorious Church happens in the corporate gathering of a local body of believers who are unified in operating the way that God has instructed. Consequently the glory also manifests in the individual believer as they mature in "sonship" because we are the Temple of God both corporately and individually.

> *"Or do you not know that your body is the temple of the Holy Spirit who is in you, whom you have from God, and you are not your own? 20 For you were bought at a price; therefore glorify God in your body and in your spirit, which are God's." 1 Corinthians 6:19-20 NKJV*

> *"having been built on the foundation of the apostles and prophets, Jesus Christ Himself being the chief cornerstone, 21 in whom the whole building, being fitted together, grows into a holy temple in the Lord," Ephesians 2:20-21 NKJV*

Wouldn't it be wonderful if everybody came to their church with a unified expectation and desire for the Glory of God, expecting miracles to happen, and for the Lord to move in their midst? Well, it is possible, but we must do things as Exodus 39 says, just as the Lord has commanded according to His pattern for building.

GOD HAS PATTERNS.

God has patterns and always works in accordance with those patterns. In fact, for you as an individual, the pattern is Jesus Christ. He's the pattern of a son and the moment you get saved, God begins to form Christ in you.

> *"But as many as received Him, to them He gave the right to become children of God, even to those who believe in His name."*
> *John 1:12 NKJV*

"Spiritual Formation" otherwise referred to as "spiritual maturity" can be understood by seeing the progression of growth in the life of Jesus Christ. There are four stages of development that we can observe in His life as a "Son" of God. These four stages of development occur in our life as Holy Spirit works in us through the revelation of the Word of God. Paul referred to this process in Galatians 4:19,

> *"My little children, for whom I labor in birth again until Christ be formed in you." Galatians 4:19 NKJV*

1. **Jesus Christ was a "saint."**

> *"For such a High Priest was fitting for us, who is holy, harmless, undefiled, separate from sinners, and has become higher than the heavens." Hebrews 7:26 NKJV*

2. **Jesus Christ was a "servant."**

> *"For even the Son of Man did not come to be served, but to serve, and to give His life a ransom for many." Mark 10:45 NKJV*

3. **Jesus Christ was a "shepherd."**

> *"I am the good shepherd. The good shepherd gives His life for the sheep." John 10:11 NKJV*

4. **Jesus Christ was a "son."**

> *"No one has seen God at any time, The*

> *only begotten Son, who is in the bosom of the Father, He has declared Him." John 1:18 NKJV*

Each of us as born again believers should look for these signs of development in our own lives as we are growing spiritually. God works according to pattern, these stages occur in consecutive order and build one upon another. God is very systematic in His work, "line upon line and precept upon precept." Isaiah 28:10

We will consider Jesus as our pattern a little later, but for now let's examine the "corporate glory" that we are talking about and see how it increases as we build according to the pattern that God lays out in scripture.

APOSTLES ARE BUILDERS

> *"Therefore, holy brethren, partakers of the heavenly calling, consider the Apostle and High Priest of our confession, Christ Jesus, who was faithful to Him who appointed Him, as Moses also was faithful in all His house. For this One has been counted worthy of more glory than Moses, inasmuch as He who built the house has more honor than the house. For every house is built by someone, but He who built*

> *all things is God. And Moses indeed was faithful in all His house as a servant, for a testimony of those things which would be spoken afterward, but Christ as a Son over His own house, whose house we are if we hold fast the confidence and the rejoicing of the hope firm to the end." Hebrews 3:1-6 NKJV*

Like Christ, who was the apostle that builds the New Testament Church, we find Moses was an apostle, who built the original tabernacle, the Old Testament Church. Let's read Exodus 39 again.

> *"The Israelites had done all the work just as the* ***Lord had commanded*** *Moses.* ***Moses inspected*** *the work and saw that they had done it just as the Lord had commanded. So,* ***Moses blessed*** *them." Exodus 39:42-43 NIV (emphasis added)*

In this scripture, we see three things: Instruction, Inspection, and Impartation. Let us take a look at each one of these in a little more detail.

APOSTOLIC INSTRUCTION

Moses didn't have his own ideas for the tabernacle,

rather he did everything God told him to do. That was the key to having the Glory of God in the church - to build according to the pattern given to him by God. This was the Apostolic Instruction. It's the first step.

> *"who serve the copy and shadow of the heavenly things, as Moses was divinely instructed when he was about to make the tabernacle. For He said, "See that you make all things according to the pattern shown you on the mountain." Hebrews 8:5 NKJV*

We must get the instruction from the apostolic leaders that God has called and given the instruction to. Look at what Paul says in 1 Corinthians,

> *"According to the grace of God which is given to me, as a wise master builder, I have laid the foundation, and another builds on it. But let each one take heed how he builds on it." 1 Corinthians 3:10 NKJV*

Here, Paul is saying he is the master builder who built according to the foundation which was Jesus Christ. This is the first step -- build according to the pattern that has been laid out by those God has called and gifted as "builders." Apostles are recognized as being "builders" while God is the "Architect." We will learn more about how the New Testament apostles built as we continue.

APOSTOLIC INSPECTION

> *"**Moses inspected** the work and saw that they had done it just as the Lord had commanded. So Moses blessed them." Exodus 39:43 NIV (emphasis added)*

Once Moses gave the instructions on how the sanctuary was to be built and the people followed those instructions, he came back and inspected it. Apostles are great inspectors of the church.

> *"For though I am absent in the flesh, yet I am with you in spirit, rejoicing to **see your good order** and the steadfastness of your faith in Christ." Colossians 2:5 NKJV (emphasis added)*

Paul wrote this to the Colossian church, which he founded. In other words, Paul inspected what he built. Jesus is also an inspector of the Church. In Revelation 2-3, He pointed out what He was pleased with and pointed out what needed to be corrected as the 1st Century Church was about to go into horrible persecution. His intention was that His Church could endure what was ahead and remain faithful witnesses.

After an inspection is done on what has been built, if it has been done according to pattern given, a blessing can then be released.

APOSTOLIC IMPARTATION

> *"Moses inspected the work and saw that they had done it just as the Lord had commanded. So **Moses blessed** them." Exodus 39:43 NIV (emphasis added)*

Once Moses inspected and confirmed that the Tabernacle was built according to the Lord's command, he blessed them. The blessing is the Glory of God, not just "good" church services, but the Manifest Presence of our Creator.

> *"Then the cloud covered the tabernacle of meeting, and the glory of the Lord filled the tabernacle." Exodus 40:34 NKJV*

> *"In all the travels of the Israelites, whenever the cloud lifted from above the tabernacle, they would set out, but if the cloud did not*

> *lift, they did not set out - - until the day it lifted." Exodus 40:36-37 NIV*

After the Glory came upon them, their journey in the supernatural began with signs, wonders and miracles. Today's Church needs the same dimension of supernatural leading and demonstration of power. If we want our churches to continually have the Glory of God, then we can't build according to our pattern, we must build according to God's pattern. We are going to see more about it in the next chapters.

SOPHISTICATION VS. DEMONSTRATION

Years ago, while involved in a Conference in the state of Michigan, I received an insight from 1 Corinthians 2:4 that turned out to be a "prophetic word."

> *"And my speech and my preaching were not with persuasive words of human wisdom, but in demonstration of the Spirit and of power." 1 Corinthians 2:4 NKJV*

The word "wisdom" in this verse is "sofia" where we get the word, 'sophistication" pertaining to "man's wisdom." Holy Spirit impressed me with this thought, "There will be two kinds of churches that emerge, the *church of sophistication* and the *church of demonstration.*" We have seen this emergence in the "seeker sensitive model' also known as the "attractional model" that is designed to make "sinners comfortable" on Sunday morning. We have seen how that model can fill seats and build mega churches, but not necessarily build "people" into mature disciples of Jesus who can "do His works" of "preaching, teaching and healing." Matthew 9:35; John 14:12-14

Following the Covid pandemic, there was a shift in the church causing a return to the biblical model of "demonstration" of the Spirit and power where sinners "*cannot stand in the congregation of the righteous.*" Psalm 1:5

We are seeing churches move back to a model that allows the move of Holy Spirit publicly, so that people can see God at work and be convicted of their sins resulting in a genuine conversion. There are multitudes in churches that have been "convicted' but never "converted" by the Spirit of God. When a person is truly born again, *"old things pass away, all things become new." 2 Corinthians 5:17*

Even "so called" Pentecostal churches look more like a mainline denominational expression than a truly spirit filled environment where the "suddenness of Spirit" occurs and people realize God is in control at the moment. Thank God, those who are sensitive to the Spirit of God are moving back to the biblical model of New Testament Christianity with supernatural manifestations taking place regularly. The "spontaneity" or "suddenness"of the Spirit moving is a characteristic of New Testament ministry.

> *"And **suddenly** there came a sound from heaven, as of a rushing mighty wind, and it filled the whole house where they were sitting." Acts 2:2 NKJV (emphasis added)*

> *"As he journeyed he came near Damascus, and **suddenly** a light shone around him from heaven." Acts 9:3 NKJV (emphasis added)*

> *"**Suddenly** there was a great earthquake, so that the foundations of the prison were shaken; and immediately all the doors were opened and everyone's chains were loosed." Acts 16:26 NKJV (emphasis added)*

GET CONNECTED

As an apostle of Christ, church planter and builder for more than 40 years, I am often called on by pastors to take a look at their church structure and government. Following the "independent church planting movement" of the 80's and beyond, many spirit filled churches were started by gifted leaders who had not received what we are referring to as "apostolic instruction" that deals with "Gifts, Government and Goals." We are now in a season whereby God is connecting leaders to "apostolic fathers" with proven ministry and loving hearts, to help church leaders align more closely to biblical principles. This often resulted in much chaos and confusion in otherwise anointed ministries. With the restoration of apostolic gifting to the Church we have seen many congregations grow strong and prosperous by building according to the pattern of Scripture.

> *"For God is not a God of disorder but of peace, as in all the congregations of the Lord's people."* 1 Corinthians 14:33 NIV

> *"But everything should be done in a fitting and orderly way."* 1 Corinthians 14:40 NIV

When apostles get involved in your life, they will help you see God's pattern. If you want the Glory of God, anything that's not in order must be put in order. The same thing is true in your individual life as a Christian. When our life does not line up to God's pattern, which is Jesus Christ, then He must help us make adjustments and many times He will use the leadership in our life to do that. He does this, not to try and control our lives, but because He loves us and wants to be able to release the fullness of His glory in and through our lives.

> *"Remember those who rule over you, who have spoken the word of God to you, whose faith follow, considering the outcome of their conduct... Obey those who rule over you, and be submissive, for they watch out for your souls, as those who must give account. Let them do so with joy and not with grief, for that would be unprofitable for you." Hebrews 13:7&17 NKJV*

In a construction site you will have the Foreman who is overseeing the actual construction, but then a "building superintendent" will come and check the construction according to the blueprint. Things must be approved before construction can continue. The

Lord does this in our lives as He is the "Chief Overseer and Shepherd of our souls." 1 Peter 2:25

> *"For you were like sheep going astray, but have now returned to the Shepherd and Overseer of your souls." 1 Peter 2:25 NKJV*

The word "Overseer" is episkopos, meaning "superintendent." The word is also translated "bishop" in Acts 20:28 and 1 Timothy 3:1. For more detail on the New Testament structure of Leadership and Government, see my book, Apostolic Advice available at johnpolis.com.

The early apostles were the "overseers" or "superintendents" of the newly formed assemblies, they were charged with inspecting the building of God's Church. The role of apostles in today's church includes this function. See my book, 9 Apostolic Functions: Things Apostles Do at johnpolis.com for a detailed explanation of apostolic responsibilities.

Chapter Two

THE GIFTS

We have learned from the Old Testament that God had a pattern for building the Tabernacle through Moses' leadership. Let's now look more closely at the New Testament Church for insights on how we are to build the church to become a "habitation" of the Glory of God.

> *"Having been built on the foundation of the apostles and prophets, Jesus Christ Himself being the chief cornerstone, in whom the whole building, being fitted together, grows into a holy temple in the Lord, in whom you also are being built*

> *together for a dwelling place of God in the Spirit." Ephesians 2:20-22 NKJV*

When you need to inspect your church, you should evaluate three things in order to have the Glory of God abide in the midst. Gifts, Government, and Goals.

Let's examine the "ministry gifts" first.

> *"So Christ himself gave the apostles, the prophets, the evangelists, the pastors and teachers, to equip his people for works of service, so that the body of Christ may be built up until we all reach unity in the faith and in the knowledge of the Son of God and become mature, attaining to the whole measure of the fullness of Christ." Ephesians 4:11-13 NIV*

Apostles, prophets, evangelists, pastors, and teachers are all gifts that Christ has given to the church to equip people for works of service. Can a local church have all five? Yes, in due time, a local church can have all five manifested.

> *"And God has placed in the church first of all apostles, second prophets, third teachers, then miracles, then gifts of*

> *healing, of helping, of guidance, and of different kinds of tongues." 1 Corinthians 12:28 NIV*

Having all five gifts in operation is really a picture of a complete apostolic team. It takes time to identify the five-fold ministry gifts and raise those gifts up in a church; but a church can have all five. That means that a local church that's going to have the Glory of God is a team ministry, not just a one-man show.

Briefly, we understand the five-fold ministry gifts have different functions within the Church.

- APOSTLES GOVERN
- PROPHETS GUIDE
- EVANGELISTS GATHER
- PASTORS GUARD
- TEACHERS GROW

When we have a compliment of these gifts in the church, either as "resident elders" or "trans local ministries" that come alongside to help the church grow, we can develop a "five-fold ministry culture." Developing a "culture" is vitally important because people can grow quickly as they are introduced to an environment where certain values and goals are shared by the group. So what would a culture based on the affect of the five-fold gifts look like? I suggest the following.

MISSION MINDED CULTURE

Apostles are usually recognized as the "missionaries" of the church since they were "sent forth" to spread the Gospel to all nations. Apostolic grace in a ministry will produce a "mission mentality" among the people. You will hear people say, "Our church is on a mission."

> *"But you shall receive power when the Holy Spirit has come upon you; and you shall be witnesses to Me in Jerusalem, and in all Judea and Samaria, and to the end of the earth." Acts 1:8 NKJV*

RELEVANT MINDED CULTURE

Prophets usually are well acquainted with what is going on the the world outside the church and can provide direction for connecting the Church in relevant terms to the world of today. Where prophetic grace is imparted in ministry, people will not be like the frog in the "frog and kettle" illustration, but will be well informed about the "world view" of people outside of Christianity.

> *"of the sons of Issachar who had understanding of the times, to know what Israel ought to do, their chiefs were two hundred; and all their brethren were at their command;" 1 Chronicles 12:32 NKJV*

HARVEST MINDED CULTURE

Evangelists are gifted to bring in the harvest of unreached people, their mind and heart is set on the unsaved people. When the grace of evangelism is released, people have their mind on the unsaved world and are looking for opportunities to share their faith.

> *"Do you not say, 'There are still four months and then comes the harvest'? Behold, I say to you, lift up your eyes and look at the fields, for they are already white for harvest!" John 4:35 NKJV*

FAMILY MINDED CULTURE

Pastors lead the church to become a "spiritual

family' by emphasizing love and care for one another. Family is the ultimate desire of our Heavenly Father, Jesus came to begin that new family of "sons and daughters."

> *"that there should be no schism in the body, but that the members should have the same care for one another." 1 Corinthians 12:25 NKJV*

GROWTH MINDED CULTURE

Teachers are "explainers of the Word" and emphasize growing to maturity in Christ. Paul said that "teaching" was "watering" the seed of the Word that has been planted in a heart.

> *"Him we preach, warning every man and teaching every man in all wisdom, that we may present every man perfect in Christ Jesus. To this end I also labor, striving according to His working which works in me mightily." Colossians 1:28-29 NKJV*

> *"I planted, Apollos watered, but God gave the increase." 1 Corinthians 3:6 NKJV*

A Local Church culture that is Mission, Relevant,

Harvest, Family, and Growth Minded will be a well balanced and healthy church that will surely grow both spiritually and numerically to influence the world around them.

THE ONE MAN SHOW

Thank God, I believe we're getting delivered from the one-man superstar model in the church! The church has allowed that model to permeate church culture due to a lack of knowledge concerning "five-fold ministry" and cessationism, the idea that many supernatural aspects of Christianity ceased during the first century of the Church.

I would liken it, the celebrity preacher model, to building your house on shifting sand like Matthew 7:26-27 talks about. But how did it gain popularity and supplant the team model of ministry. It may be because we love our celebrities. Whether they're in the musical realm, in the sports realm, or whether they're in the church realm; we love our famous people. We love to just worship man. If anything, we'll grieve the Glory of God by this celebrity worship, because it is the worship of man.

GETTING BACK TO THE PATTERN

After COVID happened in 2020, God spoke to me saying, "When you come back to church after COVID, you're not coming back the same." Here's the difference. There are two church models - we have the attractional model, and then we have the biblical model. The attractional model was the pattern used in the recent few decades to produce "church growth." We tried to make the Sunday morning service comfortable for sinners, using things such as smoke and lights to attract and entertain. Messages were more "story telling" with fewer scripture references and sought to avoid offending the listeners. I don't fault church leaders for adopting this strategy because the Church in America was not growing, individual believers were not "owning the Great Commission" and working to bring in the harvest. Consequently, church leaders developed the strategy to "attract" people to the Sunday service. We have to admit that God used this model to bring many to faith in Christ who would not have ever entered a church otherwise. But as we consider the outcomes, the believers were not doing the work of evangelism themselves, those getting saved were responding to the pastors messages. We may have conditions in the future more like those in

China and other restrictive nations where people can't assemble publicly. We must have a model that equips believers to be winning the lost daily as they interact with people outside of church services. Actually, the Sunday service shouldn't be designed for "unsaved" but for "believers" who need to be equipped to labor in the harvest fields, and to enjoy a celebration of the Savior. We are coming back!

> *"And let us consider one another in order to stir up love and good works, not forsaking the assembling of ourselves together, as is the manner of some, but exhorting one another, and so much the more as you see the Day approaching." Hebrews 10:24-25 NKJV*

> *"Praise the Lord! Praise God in His sanctuary; Praise Him in His mighty firmament! Praise Him for His mighty acts; Praise Him according to His excellent greatness! Praise Him with the sound of the trumpet; Praise Him with the lute and harp! Praise Him with the timbrel and dance; Praise Him with stringed instruments and flutes! Praise Him with loud cymbals; Praise Him with clashing*

> *cymbals! Let everything that has breath praise the Lord. Praise the Lord!" Psalm 150:1-6 NKJV*

Now, I'm not down on technology. It should be used. In fact, we utilize technology in our church, but we missed the principle here. The church is not to be a comfortable place for sinners to remain. The Bible says in Psalm 1:5, "sinners cannot stand in the congregation of the righteous". In other words, the sinner experiences conviction of the Holy Spirit from the teaching and preaching of God's Word and feels they must get rid of their sin; they will be uncomfortable in the Glory of God atmosphere. We've made the church comfortable for sinners, but it hasn't accomplished God's purpose and goals.

We've created mega churches and celebrity pastors with no transformation of the culture. That doesn't mean we are not going to have famous mega churches, and there will still be celebrity preachers, but there's a change taking place! We're getting back to the model of the New Testament church, the model of the Bible, where God has a five-fold ministry compliment based on a team of Eldership that all manifest their five-fold ministry gifts with manifestations of the Holy Spirit that have the people in awe of God. One person doesn't have it all. The saints will be equipped with the Spirit and Word to do the"works of Jesus."

> *"Most assuredly, I say to you, he who believes in Me, the works that I do he will do also; and greater works than these he will do, because I go to My Father. 13 And whatever you ask in My name, that I will do, that the Father may be glorified in the Son. 14 If you ask anything in My name, I will do it." John 14:12-14 NKJV*

> *"And when John had heard in prison about the works of Christ, he sent two of his disciples 3 and said to Him, "Are You the Coming One, or do we look for another?" 4 Jesus answered and said to them, "Go and tell John the things which you hear and see: 5 The blind see and the lame walk; the lepers are cleansed and the deaf hear; the dead are raised up and the poor have the gospel preached to them." Matthew 11:2-5 NKJV*

We're fighting an uphill battle because most churches are based upon this old and wrong model of just the pastor and the members. People will say,

"Who's the pastor?" "I want to come hear the pastor." It's all about the pastor!

PASTOR VS. SHEPHERD

In the old pattern we look for the pastor to meet all of our needs, we look for the pastor to do all the work of the ministry, we look for the pastor to do all of the visiting, and we look for the pastor to do all of the discipling. However, the word "pastor" is only used two times in the King James Version of the New Testament. "Apostle/Apostles/Apostles'" is used seventy-nine times! Prophet/prophets/prophet's is mentioned 482 times; teacher/teachers is named in nineteen instances. The "gifted leaders" are "trainers" while the "saints" are the "laborers in the harvest.

> *"And He Himself gave some to be apostles, some prophets, some evangelists, and some pastors and teachers, for the equipping of the saints for the work of ministry, for the edifying of the body of Christ," Ephesians 4:11-12 NKJV*

> *"Then Jesus went about all the cities and villages, teaching in their synagogues, preaching the gospel of the kingdom,*

> *and healing every sickness and every disease among the people. But when He saw the multitudes, He was moved with compassion for them, because they were weary and scattered, like sheep having no shepherd. Then He said to His disciples, "The harvest truly is plentiful, but the laborers are few. Therefore pray the Lord of the harvest to send out laborers into His harvest."" Matthew 9:35-38 NKJV*

Since Christ is our pattern in the New Testament we must model our lives after His. He was a Saint, a Servant, a Shepherd, and a Son. If we are patterning ourselves after Christ then all of these things will be formed in us as well. We are to be...

- **A saint**: holy and set apart for God's purpose.
- **A servant**: ready to do whatever God needs us to do.
- **A shepherd**: laying down our lives for others.
- **A son**: who is always about the father's buisness and representing Him.

Everyone does not have a pastoral gift to lead a church, but we should all have a shepherd's heart where we are caring for and laying our lives down for one another. More than 100 times in Scripture the phrase "one another" is used to describe all aspects of the relationships and responsibilities believers have together.

To try and do things the old way is like what a mentor of mine used to say, "*it's like taking a bath with your socks on.*" It doesn't feel right. If you are trying to flow with the Holy Spirit and trying to do it according to the old model, it will not work. We must get back to the pattern, the Bible pattern and we will experience the genuine move of God that will reach the masses.

Chapter Three

STRAYING FROM THE PATTERN

In 1 Chronicles, 13 through 17, we learn of King David and the Ark of the Covenant. The ark was the symbol of God's glory and Presence, David wanted to bring it to Jerusalem because of his hunger and passion for the Presence and Glory of God. As they were transporting it on a cart, two men, Uzzah and Ahio were guiding it. Neither of these men were priests according to requirements for carrying the ark.

> *"They moved the ark of God from Abinadab's house on a new cart, with*

> *Uzzah and Ahio guiding it. David and all the Israelites were celebrating with all their might before God, with songs and with harps, lyres, timbrels, cymbals, and trumpets. When they came to the threshing floor of Kidon, Uzzah reached out his hand to steady the ark, because the oxen stumbled. The Lord's anger burned against Uzzah, and he struck him down because he had put his hand on the ark. So he died there before God. Then David was angry because the Lord's wrath had broken out against Uzzah, and to this day the place is called Perez Uzzah." 1 Chronicles 13:7-11 NIV*

When people start dying in service, leadership will get shook up! What does it take for us to check out our strategy and make some changes!

Many years ago, a man died during a Sunday morning service, and it got my attention! We were having an unusual Sunday morning experience; the devil was trying everything to keep us from experiencing the purpose of corporate gathering. The praise team did a good job, but the people weren't responding. I took over and still, nothing. I thought,

"*Well I'm going to try to preach this message anyway,*" so I began to speak, and it was like the people weren't even there; they certainly weren't plugged into the Spirit but seemed to be bound by a spirit of fear.

Suddenly, Sister Lily yelled out "*Pastor Polis!*" Her husband, CJ, had collapsed in the pew. There was a nurse present; she couldn't find any pulse...he was gone. The Spirit of God came on me like Elijah when he outran the king's chariot. I jumped over the altar rail, ran back to where he was, climbing over three or four people to reach him. I put my hand on him and said, "*I command the spirit of death to come out!*" He awoke, got up, and began walking around. Praise God! However, when the nurse had stated he had no pulse, one of the ushers had called 911. In no time at all, the ambulance arrived with attendants rushing into the sanctuary looking for a dead man. What they found was CJ, walking around, drinking a glass of water, with a strong pulse! As you can imagine, the power of God fell on the church. Everyone was on their feet singing "Power In The Blood." That story doesn't really fit in the narrative, but it's interesting anyway!

> *"David was afraid of God that day, saying, "How can I bring the ark of God to me?" So*

> *David would not move the ark with him into the City of David, but took it aside into the house of Obed-Edom the Gittite. The ark of God remained with the family of Obed-Edom in his house three months. And the Lord blessed the house of Obed-Edom and all that he had." 1 Chronicles 13:12-14 NKJV*

Returning to scripture, King David didn't want people dying in service anymore! He, in essence, said, "*Hold it right there!*" It's also interesting to note that for the next three months that the ark remained where he left it. Because of God's glory on the ark, Obed-Edom's household and everything he had, was blessed...where the Glory of the Lord resides, blessings abound!

David did his research; he went back and read the books of Moses regarding the proper handling of the ark. He found out how the ark was to be transported and arranged for it to be done according to the perscribed pattern.

> *"David built houses for himself in the City of David; and he prepared a place for the ark of God, and pitched a tent for it. Then David said, 'No one may carry the ark*

> *of God but the Levites, for the Lord has chosen them to carry the ark of God and to minister before Him forever.'"* 1 Chronicles 15:1-2 NIV

> *"It was because you, the Levites, did not bring it up the first time that the Lord our God broke out in anger against us. We did not inquire of him about how to do it in the prescribed way." ... "And the Levites carried the ark of God with the poles on their shoulders, as Moses had commanded in accordance with the work of the Lord."* 1 Chronicles 15:13 & 15 NIV

There is a prescribed manner for doing things the way God wants them done. We need to do WHAT God wants the WAY God wants it done. We must understand the difference between complete obedience and partial obedience to God. We're talking about building according to the pattern, doing things God's way.

When Jesus died ... can you imagine if He would've said, "*I'm willing to die, because I know You need Me to die, but I want to die a different way.*"

> *"Rather, he (Jesus) made himself nothing by taking the very nature of a servant,*

> *being made in human likeness. And being found in appearance as a man, he humbled himself by becoming obedient to death - - even death on a cross!" Philippians 1:7-8 NIV*

Jesus did what God wanted; the way God wanted it done. It wouldn't have been the same had He done it a different way. It wasn't just a matter of "Oh well, as long as He died." No, He had to be crucified to fulfill the prophetic word of God. We must do what God wants, but we first must find out how God wants us to do it. We just can't do God's work any old way we want, that is why churches are in a mess many times, because they say, "God wants to start a church," and then they go about doing it without learning about God's pattern for building. But if we would first find out the instruction, perform the inspection, and experience the approval impartation, we will have a ministry that has history and legacy.

> *"You did not choose Me, but I chose you and appointed you that you should go and bear fruit, and that your fruit should remain, that whatever you ask the Father*

in My name He may give you." John 15:16 NKJV

Chapter Four

BUILDING TEAM MINISTRY

One of the ways to get back to the pattern of the five-fold ministry in the church is by building a 'teaching team." Instead of the same person week in and week out behind the pulpit, you have different voices with different gifts, sharing different stories and illustrations that bring a fresh perspective of the Word of God. This is not to say that the "lead pastor/elder" shouldn't have ample time in the pulpit, the people still need to hear the "voice of the shepherd."(quote from Apostle John Kelly)

As a warning with this model, don't make the mistake of putting people into the pulpit before they are ready. Jesus never gave authority to anybody in His ministry but His own disciples. Until the people you are training are truly your disciples, don't let them near that pulpit. Your disciple will understand "your ways in Christ" and not deviate from them. Paul referred to Timothy in this regard.

> *"For this reason I have sent Timothy to you, who is my beloved and faithful son (disciple) in the Lord, who will remind you of my ways in Christ, as I teach everywhere in every church. 1 Corinthians 4:15-17 NKJV*

In an apostolic ministry, you will know who your real disciples are when they have learned to know your vision, your values, and the victories in your life. They know what you stand for and what the corporate mission and core values are of the house of God they serve in.

When you give somebody the pulpit, you give them a sword. The Word of God is a like a two-edged sword (Hebrews 4:12). Before you give anybody that kind of power and authority, you need to know whether they're going to fight for you or against you with it. All too often in churches, because we're in a hurry, we put the sword in people's hand prematurely and they start cutting off ears like Peter did when Jesus was being arrested (Matthew 26:51, Mark 14:47, Luke 22:50-51, and John 10-1). Zealous, un-discipled, pulpit-fillers are going to destroy the people and prevent them from hearing, because they do not yet have the heart of God in their preaching and teaching. So many churches have been destroyed because people didn't wait on the Lord to raise up people through a process of making disciples.

I can honestly say, “Thank God,” we have a great team at our church, but it has taken years to get where we are. One of the great qualities of a leader is that you must be long-suffering and have a lot of patience or you’ll never make it. We have a teaching team of disciples who have a blend of five-fold ministry gifts. I can put any one of those elders in the pulpit and nobody is disappointed. I don't even have to be there to hear it because I know who they are and know what's in them. We've taken time to train them, to get to know one other personally, and to form the leader/disciple relationship. They are all truly my disciples, so they can be trusted. Take the time to study the five-fold ministry gifts, then teach the five-fold ministry, what they are and how they operate, and then make disciples. Don't put people behind the pulpit because they are "anointed". They qualify and earn that position first by exemplifying the doctrines of the Word of God, their lives are a living example that others can follow, and then knowing and living the vision of the church. Do not promote the gifts in someone's life, promote their character.

After Peter hacked off a man's ear, spiritual speaking he destroyed the man's hearing, Jesus as the mature spiritual father was able to bring healing and restore the man's ability to listen to God again. When we allow immature but gifted people who haven't yet really "known the Lord intimately" in the pulpit, someone may have a new ministry of "healing ears."

> *"But Jesus answered, 'No more of this!' And He touched the man's ear and healed him." Luke 22:51 NIV*

It will take the mature father in the house to heal what the immature preacher does.

Chapter Five

GOVERNMENT

The government of the church is taught by Paul throughout the New Testament. These teachings from Galatians, Romans, Corinthians, Philemon, Philippians, Thessalonians, Timothy, Titus, Ephesians, and Colossians are called the Pastoral Epistles. I prefer to refer to them as Apostolic Epistles because they were written by an apostle to an apostle, and they teach the order of the church. It was the apostles who determined the qualifications for leadership. They're the ones who taught what the "two offices"of ministry were in the New Testament, namely the Deacons and the Elders.

An "office" is an "official function". Just because someone has a "gift" doesn't make them a church official. Anointing doesn't qualify you for authority in the church. What qualifies you is your maturity. That's why you have qualifications for leadership in 1 Timothy 3:1-13, Titus 1:5-9 and Acts 6:3-4, where they teach on the qualities of Deacons and Elders. None of these passages talk about how gifted a person is because the focus is on the character of the individual. It's all character development. Why? Because it requires "qualifications to produce quality". In order for the church to produce "high quality believers" there must first be "high quality leadership." This will take time and process to produce. In my local churches, we have three stage process designed to transform "believers into disciples."

We first become an attender in the church, then we become a member in the church, then we become a leader in the church. This follows the logical pattern of growth from Mark 4:28,

> *"For the earth yields crops by itself: first the blade, then the head, after that the full grain in the head." Mark 4:28 NKJV*

You do not start with the "full grain in the head" it

is only through the process of time and maturity that this is produced.

We see this pattern of growth to maturity throughout the Bible with the number three. Everything in the kingdom is in three phases; babyhood, childhood, and manhood; Jesus, Holy Spirit, Father; outer court, inner court, holiest of all; first the blade, then the head, after that the full grain in the head. You must have that three-step process in your church for raising people up, attender, then member, then leader. It's a process.

FOLLOW THE LEADER

> *"'Come, follow me,' Jesus said, 'and I will send you out to fish for people.'"* Matthew 4:19 NIV

According to this verse, Jesus had a three stage process beginning with

1. "Come Follow Me" - I will be the pattern for you to follow.
2. "I Will Make You To Become" - This will be a process to complete.
3. "Fishers Of Men" - The product will result.

Paul also had a process for his would be "sons" in ministry were to follow.

> *"But I trust in the Lord Jesus to send Timothy to you shortly, that I also may be encouraged when I know your state. For I have no one like-minded, who will sincerely care for your state. For all seek their own, not the things which are of Christ Jesus. But you know his proven character, that as a son with his father he served with me in the gospel. Therefore I hope to send him at once, as soon as I see how it goes with me." Philippians 2:19-23 NKJV*

You may have other people influencing your life, but you will have only one spiritual father in your life at a time, that you make yourself accountable to. I have only one spiritual father in my life, ours is a father/son relationship that has been established; I'm not looking at anybody else for what only he can do in my life. I may have a multitude of teachers who can coach and mentor me, but "spiritual fathers" are those you entrust yourself to for personal and private issues because you know they love you and can be trusted.

BACK TO JESUS

"On hearing it, many of his disciples said, 'This is a hard teaching. Who can accept it?'" ... "For this time many of his disciples turned back and no longer followed him. 'You do not want to leave too, do you?' Jesus asked the Twelve. Simon Peter answered him 'Lord, to whom shall we go? You have the words of eternal life. We have come to believe and to know that you are the Holy One of God.'" John 6:60 & 66-69 NIV

In this scripture, people were leaving Jesus because He said some difficult things to understand which could only be grasped by revelation of the Spirit, which came later. Because they didn't understand, instead of drawing closer to Him to get understanding, they turned their backs and left. As they were leaving, Jesus asks the twelve disciples if they are going to leave also, and Peter answered clearly with understanding that only Jesus had the words of eternal life; through Him they came to believe and know that He was the Holy One of God. In other words, Jesus was their mentor, coach, apostle, trainer, spiritual father, and the one raising them to maturity. They realized His words were different than others. They had access to many teachers, but nobody could do what He did in their lives. His words were "spirit and life" (John 6:63). God's words, through your spiritual father, brings revelation and impartation, spirit and life.

SIFTING SONS

Revelation and impartation come from the God-appointed leadership in your life. That's why you need to guard that relationship, Satan will try to separate you from them. It's called "being sifted."

> *"And the Lord said, "Simon, Simon! Indeed, Satan has asked for you, that he may sift you as wheat. But I have prayed for you, that your faith fail not; and when you have returned to Me, strengthen your brethren."*
> *Luke 22:31-32 NKJV*

Satan will try to separate you from the people God puts in your life to raise you up, to coach you, to lead you, to bring you to maturity. Anybody can make a baby, but it takes a mature person to raise that baby to adulthood. Your spiritual parents are not there to dictate to you or control your life. They're there for your maturation and development into Christlikeness.

Parents raise children. Regardless of how this has been misguided in our modern society, it doesn't change the fact that parents are responsible to raise their children, just as spiritual fathers/mothers are responsible for maturing the next generation of Christians.

A PROCESS TO MATURITY

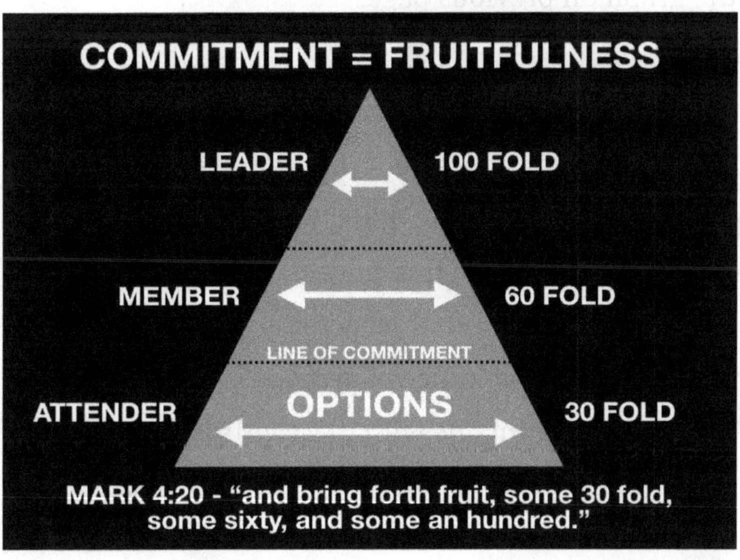

You must have a process in your church to bring people from being an attender, to member, to leader. When people reach the "leadership stage" they will be ready for an "Office" such as Deacon or Elder. By the time you get people all the way through that process, you've got somebody ready that can publicly release their gift to the Body of Christ. In the meantime, people can use their giftings privately and we should do so, everywhere we go. At work, at school, whatever and wherever, let God use you. But when it comes to officially having authority within the local church, that requires release from your leadership with qualifications and validation. Progressing through stages to "fruitfulness" will require "commitment." See the graph on previous page.

TWO OFFICIAL FUNCTIONS

As mentioned before, I believe scripture teaches a difference between "gifts and offices."There are differing opinions on this subject, I will offer mine. We often hear the five-fold leadership gifts of Ephesians 4:11 referred to as "office of prophet", "office of pastor" indicating that anyone with these gifts is automatically a "church official", someone in authority within the local church. An "office" is an "official function", as in "church officers." My view is all those with "a five-fold ministry gift" do not automatically become an authority figure in the church. This is what Paul warned Timothy about, "*Lay hands suddenly (too soon) on no man; neither be partaker of other men's sins; keep yourself pure." 1 Timothy 5:22*

God gives "gifts and callings" before a person is

matured enough to be given authority over other believers. I wish it was the other way around but it isn't, like Jeremiah who was called as "prophet to the nations" before he was born. I wish God would wait to give Gifts and Callings until after a person is matured and can be an "example to the flock of God." His obvious plan is to give gifts first and then use the gift and calling to test a person's humility or pride.

When we are aware that we have certain gifts and callings and "submit ourselves to others for training and release" we qualify for promotion to function "officially" within the church.

> *"Likewise you younger people, submit yourselves to your elders. Yes, all of you be submissive to one another, and be clothed with humility, for "God resists the proud, but gives grace to the humble." Therefore humble yourselves under the mighty hand of God, that He may exalt you in due time," 1 Peter 5:5-6 NKJV*

GIFTS OR OFFICES

We know what the "gifts" are, but what about the "offices?"

> *"This is a faithful saying: If a man desires the position of a bishop, he desires a good work." 1 Timothy 3:1 NKJV*

> *"But let these also first be tested; then let them serve as deacons, being found blameless." 1 Timothy 3:10 NKJV*

First, let's consider the term "bishop." The word "episkope" means "inspection, superintendence" according to Strong's Concordance G1984 and is used to describe the "function of an Elder." The term, "bishop and elder" both refer to the same person in scripture as recorded in Acts 20:17, 28.

> *"From Miletus he sent to Ephesus and called for the elders of the church." Acts 20:17 NKJV*

> *"Therefore take heed to yourselves (elders) and to all the flock, among which the Holy Spirit has made you overseers, to shepherd the church of God which He purchased with His own blood." Acts 20:28 NKJV*

The term "Elder" is translated from "presbuteros" meaning "a senior, elderly, older." When Paul called the leaders of the Ephesian church together, he called for the "elders", not "bishops" because "elders" were the spiritual leaders of the New Testament Church and were "ordained" by the apostles in all the churches.

> *"So when they had appointed elders in every church, and prayed with fasting, they commended them to the Lord in whom they had believed." Acts 14:23 NKJV*

> *"They wrote this letter by them: The apostles, the elders, and the brethren, To the brethren who are of the Gentiles in Antioch, Syria, and Cilicia: Greetings." Acts 15:23 NKJV*

The term "elder" refers to the spiritual "maturity' of the person while "bishop" refers to their "function." But both terms refer to the same person as we can readily see in Acts 20:28 and were not intended to be separated into two different "official functions."

Here Paul is speaking to the "elders" he had called together and is outlining their "job description" as follows...

> *"Take heed to therefore to yourselves, and to all the flock, over which the Holy*

> *Ghost hath made you overseers (bishop), to feed the church of God, which he hath purchased with his own blood." Acts 20:28 KJV*

Elders are to supervise (oversee/bishop) the work of ministry and feed/teach the flock of God. The title used for church officials was "Elder", not "Bishop." The idea of "bishops" becoming an official position came years later after the Church became more of an institution than an organism. For a detailed study of the development of Apostles and Bishops in the NT, see From Apostles to Bishops: A Study of the Development of Christendom by Dr. Ronald Cottle. (Available on Amazon)

CLASSIFICATION OF ELDERS

> *"Let the elders that rule well be counted worthy of double honour, especially they who labour in the word and doctrine." 1 Timothy 5:17 NKJV*

Here we see "ruling elders" and "teaching elders." Both functions can be done by the same person, but there are different graces for different assignments. Some elders are more gifted at "administration" and can "rule well" while others are more gifted at "teaching/preaching the Word of God." Regardless of the function, the elder is one who has met the character qualifications and been publicly recognized and set (ordained) into the "office." In my view, "authority comes from the office not the anointing."

Gifting brings anointing, maturity brings wisdom! That is why we don't make "officials" based upon gifting only, wait for "maturity and wisdom" before releasing "gifting." The New Testament apostle ordained "character not anointing."

> *"The fear of the Lord is the instruction of wisdom, And before honor is humility." Proverbs 15:33 NKJV*

> *"serving the Lord with all humility, with many tears and trials which happened to me by the plotting of the Jews;" Acts 20:19 NKJV*

WHAT ABOUT DEACONS

The only other "office" or "official function" mentioned in the New Testament is that of the "deacon." The word means "an attendant" and "servant" referring to those who assisted the Elders in the performance of duties other than "prayer and public ministry of the Word of God."

> *"Now in those days, when the number of the disciples was multiplying, there arose a complaint against the Hebrews by the Hellenists, because their widows were neglected in the daily distribution. Then the twelve summoned the multitude of the disciples and said, "It is not desirable that we should leave the word of God and serve tables. Therefore, brethren, seek out from among you seven men of good reputation, full of the Holy Spirit and wisdom, whom we may appoint over this business; but we will give ourselves continually to prayer and to the ministry of the word." Acts 6:1-4 NKJV*

However, the New Testament Deacon was a spirit filled believer that operated in the supernatural "among the people." I call them "dynamic deacons." The Eldership was "over the people" (Hebrews 13:7), while Deacons were "among the people." An important distinctive!

> *"And Stephen, full of faith and power,*

> *did great wonders and signs among the people." Acts 6:8 NKJV*

Notice that even while these Dynamic Deacons did miracles while serving the people, they remained under the authority of the Eldership. Deacons that served well were often elevated to the position of Elders and could rule over the people and publicly minister the Word of God in the assemblies.

> *"For those who have served well as deacons obtain for themselves a good standing and great boldness in the faith which is in Christ Jesus." 1 Timothy 3:13 NKJV*

In Paul's letter to the Philippians, he sends greetings to three groups of people, "saints, bishops and deacons." It was understood that Paul and Timothy were "apostles" serving the church. It was also understood that the "bishops" were the locally ordained Elders of the church. Here they are being referred to by their "function" not by an "office."

> *"Paul and Timothy, bondservants of Jesus Christ, To all the saints in Christ Jesus who are in Philippi, with the bishops and deacons:" Philippians 1:1 NKJV*

So how do we refer to the Five-Fold gifts of Ephesians 4:11? I prefer to call them what the Bible calls them, "gifts."

> *"Therefore He says: "When He ascended on high, He led captivity captive, And gave gifts to men." Ephesians 4:8 NKJV*

Chapter Six

THE GOAL

The local church pattern is based on three things. You must have the 3G's - - Gifts, Government, and then you must have a Goal.

> *"Then the eleven disciples went to Galilee, to the mountain where Jesus had told them to go. When they saw him, they worshiped him; but some doubted. Then Jesus came to them and said, 'All authority in heaven and on earth has been given to me. Therefore go and make disciples of all nations, baptizing them in the name of the Father and of the Son and of the*

> *Holy Spirit, and teaching them to obey everything I have commanded you. And surely I am with you always, to the very end of the age.'" Matthew 28:16-20 NIV*

What is the goal? Jesus gave us the goal, the Great Commission, to "go and make disciples of all nations." We must first make believers, then take those believers and turn them into disciples, and then help them become disciple-makers themselves. We need disciple-makers in the church. God spoke to me saying, *"Train your teachers and your preachers, You're going to need a lot of help to disciple this harvest that's going to come in ... this massive harvest."*

Have you seen the Jesus Revolution movie? This movie portrayed a move of God, a national spiritual awakening in the early 1970's. Other spiritual awakenings are coming in our future, but the real question is are we going to be ready for it? If we're doing church as usual, we aren't going to be ready? The goals of your church should be the goals that Jesus gave us. Not just church growth, not just filling seats, not just a bigger building budget. All of those things will naturally happen when we focus on getting people saved and getting people discipled. Numeric growth only is the wrong goal, our goal which is salvation and discipleship goes back to the dominion mandate.

> *"Then God said, 'Let us make mankind in our image, in our likeness, so that they may rule over the fish in the sea and the birds in the sky, over the livestock and all the wild animals, and over all the creatures that move along the ground.' So God created mankind in his own image, in the image of God he created them; male and female he created them. God blessed them and said to them, 'Be fruitful and increase in number; fill the earth and subdue it. Rule over the fish in the sea and the birds in the sky and over every living creature that moves on the ground.'" Genesis 1:26-28 NIV*

It is important to note that this dominion mandate, to spread the Garden of Eden to the whole world, was before the fall of man. Adam and Eve, the original "dream team," ruined the original plan but God's dream never dies because it's the Word of God, even though the dream team can fail. God's dream never dies, but He may need another dream team to be raised up to accomplish it. Like the children of Israel, they were all called to go into the Promised Land, but the first dream team died in the wilderness. Joshua started over with a new team, they got into the vision, they got into the Promised Land. The dream never changes, but the dream team did.

That has worked in my own life. I fulfilled somebody else's dream when I came to Fairmont, West Virginia. I initially knew nothing about it, but I was heading a new "dream team" along with the people God raised up to work with me. We have fulfilled a dream that was given to the original founder of the First Pentecostal Church of Fairmont back in the 1950s. They all died off and didn't fulfill it. I came in 1980 and God put that same dream in my heart though I had never heard it or knew about it. We did everything that the man was led to do, but the people, at that time, wouldn't let him do it. One of the older members of the church at age 87, came to me and said, *"I've been here from the mud hole to the roof."* He took me up in the attic and showed me the rafters that were hand-hewn, informing me that he brought them from the log mill himself. He said, *"Everything you're doing now is what Brother So and So wanted to do, the founder of the church; he wanted to do those same things."* Thirty years later, Rebecca and I came along and did every one of them.

God's dream never dies! His dream doesn't change, but the dream team can. The church may have defaulted in the dream. That's why our culture is the way it is, but God's dream never dies and a whole new team is going to be raised up to fulfill the dream! So, you must have the gifts, the government and the goals. Evaluate your church. Make sure that you are lined up with the scripture. God will complete His plan for Earth and Heaven!

> *"But the day of the Lord will come as a thief in the night, in which the heavens will pass away with a great noise, and the elements will melt with fervent heat; both the earth and the works that are in it will be burned up. Therefore, since all these things will be dissolved, what manner of persons ought you to be in holy conduct and godliness, looking for and hastening the coming of the day of God, because of which the heavens will be dissolved, being on fire, and the elements will melt with fervent heat?" 2 Peter 3:10-12 NKJV*

Chapter Seven

THE GLORY IN YOU

"I keep asking that the God of our Lord Jesus Christ, the glorious Father, may give you the Spirit of wisdom and revelation, so that you may know him better. I pray that the eyes of your heart may be enlightened in order that you may know the hope to which he has called you, the riches of his glorious inheritance in his holy people, and his incomparably great power for us who believe. That power is the same as the mighty strength he exerted when he raised Christ from the dead and seated him at his right hand in the heavenly

> *realms, far above all rule and authority, power and dominion, and every name that is invoked, not only in the present age but also in the one to come. And God placed all things under his feet and appointed him to be head over everything for the church, which is his body, the fullness of him who fills everything in every way." Ephesians 1:17-23 NIV*

> *"In bringing many sons and daughters to glory, it was fitting that God, for whom and through whom everything exists, should make the pioneer of their salvation perfect through what he suffered. Both the one who makes people holy and those who are made holy are of the same family. So Jesus is not ashamed to call them brothers and sisters. He says, 'I will declare your name to my brothers and sisters; in the assembly I will sing your praises.'" Hebrews 2:10-12 NIV*

God is the Father of Glory. He's going to bring many sons and daughters to glory. We've got a glorious future ahead of us. We used to all say this in the old Pentecostal church. "*When we die and get to glory, I'm in that way, that glory land way!"* They were probably referring to our glorified bodies after we die, but the Bible teaches glory is not only after we die, but is here, now, in us.

> *"And we know that all things work together for good to those who love God, to those who are the called according to His purpose. For whom He foreknew, He also predestined to be conformed to the image of His Son, that He might be the firstborn among many brethren.* ***Moreover whom He predestined, these He also called; whom He called, these He also justified; and whom He justified, these He also glorified."*** *Romans 8:28-30 NKJV (emphasis added)*

You have been glorified! The glory is in your spirit; Christ in you, the hope (possibility) of glory. The Bible tells us we have hope; hope is possibility. It's possible for us to live and walk in that glory now! Christ in you is the hope of glory. Previously, we could not attain to the Glory of God because of having a spiritual nature of incompatibility with God. Our sinful nature separated us from God, we could encounter God's Glory in our soul realm while in an anointed service, but the Glory could not come into our spirits until we became born again.

> *"For all have sinned and fall short of the glory of God" Romans 3:23 NIV*

As New Creations in Christ we can now enter and live in the ever increasing Glory of God in our lives.

> *"Now the Lord is the Spirit; and where the Spirit of the Lord is, there is liberty. But we all, with unveiled face, beholding as in a mirror the glory of the Lord, are being transformed into the same image from glory to glory, just as by the Spirit of the Lord." 2 Corinthians 3:17-18 NKJV*

We can go from one degree of glory to another, but how does that happen? It happens as we grow from babyhood to childhood to manhood? Every level of growth has another degree of glory to it. It's all about growing up spiritually. It's all about becoming mature sons and daughters.

THE THREE LEVELS OF THE TABERNACLE

As I had mentioned before, the number three appears throughout God's Word as a sign of maturity.

We see this in the three courts of the Old Testament Tabernacle, the outer court, inner court, and holy of holies. The outer court can symbolize the anointing within you. The inner court, the anointing upon you. The third court, the holy of holies contains the Glory. These three courts parallel the stages of maturity, babyhood, childhood, manhood. The third court, or the full maturity stage, is the harvest stage that results from the Glory of God manifested in your life. This also parallels the three stages of agricultural growth as told in The Parable of The Growing Seed, mentioned earlier, and here in NIV version:

> *"He also said, 'This is what the kingdom of God is like. A man scatters seed on the ground. Night and day, whether he sleeps or gets up, the seed sprouts and grows, though he does not know how. All by itself the soil produces grain—first the stalk, then the head, then the full kernel in the head. As soon as the grain is ripe, he puts the sickle to it, because the harvest has come.'" Mark 4:26-29 NIV*

The most fruitful time of your life is going to be the most mature time of your life, but it does take "time" to get there. That's why we often see people that are chronologically in their 60s to 70s being the most productive because of the level of maturity they have been able to reach.

We must be always growing in the revelation of sonship, becoming maturing sons and daughters of God. Paul gives some very clear teaching on the importance and results of growing out of childhood as a believer.

> *"When I was a child, I spoke as a child, I understood as a child, I thought as a child; but when I became a man, I put away childish things." 1 Corinthians 13:11 NKJV*

Some childish traits...

> *"Therefore, laying aside all malice, all deceit, hypocrisy, envy, and all evil speaking, as newborn babes, desire the pure milk of the word, that you may grow thereby," 1 Peter 2:1-2 NKJV*

> *"And now these three remain: faith, hope and love. But the greatest of these is love." 1 Corinthians 13:13 NIV*

The observable qualities of a mature son and

daughter of God are Faith, Hope, and Love. The greatest of these is love. In the parallel of the tabernacle, faith is in the outer court, hope is in the inner court and love is behind that veil, in the holy of holies where the Glory dwells. Everything behind that veil is the third dimension, or where the mature believer lives and walks.

Another analogy: The outer court is thanksgiving. The inner court is praise. The Holy of holies is worship. All those third-dimension qualities are the characteristics of a mature believer. The mature are the true worshipers we refer to as having "perfection/ completion." Sonship is immediate at the New Birth, but growth to maturity is not instant but a process. Maturity brings Glory!

> *"To them God willed to make known what are the riches of the glory of this mystery among the Gentiles: which is Christ in you, the hope of Glory. Him we preach, warning every man and teaching every man in all wisdom, that we may present every man perfect in Christ Jesus. To this end I also labor, striving according to His working which works in me mightily." Colossians 1:27-29 NKJV*

The key to getting into that third dimension is to get beyond the veil. When Christ died, the temple veil was "rent in twain, from top to bottom" (Matthew 27:51 KJV). It's symbolic. You and I have a separating veil. It's called the veil of the flesh, often expressed by an orphan independent spirit that we inherited from Adam. Remember that Jesus addressed this issue to fallen man,

> *"I will not leave you orphans; I will come to you." John 14:18*

THE ORPHAN INDEPENDENT SPIRIT

So what is an orphan independent spirit? It is a remainder from our sin nature, causing a sense of abandonment, that affects the mind and emotions. We all became separated from God by sin and experienced the feeling of abandonment and proceeded to guide our own lives apart from God. It is common in people who have experienced extreme rejection or abandonment especially from a father figure. Whether the dad left the home purposely because of divorce or some other reason, or the father may have even passed away, the feelings of abandonment are still there. The orphan independent spirit forms because the child has to do for themselves what a parent should have done for them. Essentially, they parent themselves. What does that involve? What should a parent do for the child? There are many things of course, but among the most important are to,

- Provide
- Protect
- Promote
- Pattern

When a child is left to themselves, they develop an independent spirit that says, "*I don't need anyone, I can take care of myself.*" Unfortunately, when someone becomes a Christian with a background of orphan/independence, they will carry these traits into their new life in Christ.

It is a spiritual stronghold. It is a false mindset, a lie from satan, that makes us feel unloved and unaccepted, and does not align with the truth of God's Word that states we are individually loved and accepted.

This stronghold of, "*I don't need anybody.*" "*I can do this myself*" manifests even after salvation by falsely thinking "*I have the Holy Spirit.*" "*I have the Bible.*" "*I don't need anyone else." "I don't need a spiritual father or mother; I can be a Christian all by myself."* Many new believers have this mindset that needs to be adjusted through the teaching of God's Word.

Christianity doesn't work that way because it is the "family of God." This means we must learn to have healthy and productive relationships with one another, including how we relate to spiritual "mothers and fathers" in our lives. The stronghold of orphan/independence in our lives will lead to "self promotion", "self protection", "self provision". This strong "self led" lifestyle is the "veil of the flesh" that must be "rent from top to bottom" by the Spirit of God as we learn to entrust ourselves to more mature leaders that can help guide us in our spiritual journey to Christlikeness. The Local Church is designed by God to be "family of believers" where there are those who have developed the "heart of the Father" and can become "spiritual parents" to newer believers. God has promised this restoration of relationship in the Old Testament.

> *"And he will turn the hearts of the fathers to the children, and the hearts of the children to their fathers, lest I come and*

strike the earth with a curse." Malachi 4:6 NKJV

God will connect you in relationship with spiritually mature leadership. You have to start allowing them to parent you spiritually. You have to start allowing them to promote you, protect you, and provide for you, and be a pattern for you feeding you the Word of God. Only when you allow spiritual parenting in your life, will you be free from the Orphan Independent Spirit. You can't cast it out; just like the veil that separated the holy of holies from the other compartments, it must be torn from "top to bottom" signifying that it is a work done by God. This veil of "independence" that refuses to allow "intimate" spiritual relationships in the Body of Christ, also hinders us from "intimacy" with our Father God. When the "veil is rent" we come to a new place of understanding God's Love for us, we are able to receive it and give it to others.

Someone has rightly stated, *"The biggest problem a person has, is whatever hinders them from receiving and giving the Love of God."*

THE I THAT MUST DIE.

One day while meditating on Galatians 2:20, I was quickened with this thought, "The I that must die."

> *"I have been crucified with Christ; it is no longer I who live, but Christ lives in me; and the life which I now live in the flesh I live by faith in the Son of God, who loved me and gave Himself for me." Galatians 2:20 NKJV*

I saw three "I's" that needed to "die" in my life also in order to make room from Christ to live His life through me, as Paul said. Here they are for your consideration.

- Independence - I have the Spirit and Bible, I don't need anyone to teach me.
- Ignorance - I am not interested in learning any more, I'm saved.
- Isolation - I don't really care to connect with others, I'm not a people person.

These three traits are characteristic of the "self life" that Jesus referred to in Matthew 16:24.

> *"Then Jesus said to His disciples, "If*

anyone desires to come after Me, let him deny himself, and take up his cross, and follow Me." Matthew 16:24 NKJV

The Third Dimension Qualities of a mature son and daughter of God that we should see developing as we grow are,

- Anointing Within, Anointing Upon, **Glory of God**.
- Faith, Hope, **Love**.
- Thanksgiving, Praise, **Worship**.
- Praying in English, Praying in Tongues, **Groan/ Travail**.
- Babyhood, Childhood, **Manhood**.
- Jesus, Holy Spirit, **Father**.
- Blade, Corn, Full Corn/**Harvest**.

Coming into the Holy Of Holies and dwelling there is not the result of "hands laid upon someone" or "sowing a special seed", but of actual growth through the process to spiritual maturity as sons and daughters of Father God.

Chapter Eight

THE GLORIOUS CHURCH

> *"That he might present her to himself a glorious church, not having spot or wrinkle or any such thing, but that she should be holy and without blemish." Ephesians 5:27 NKJV*

In this scripture, we are compared to a glorious bride...the church, now having come to the same measure of glory that the bridegroom is walking in, into the maturity of sons. We've become compatible with our Bridegroom, Christ. What makes you compatible with "the Bridegroom?" You're carrying the same glory that He's carrying. This is why I don't believe the rapture is going to happen very soon, because we've got a long way to go. I don't know how long it's going to be, but the corporate church has got to get to the same degree of Glory that Christ walked in during His earthly ministry.

THE TRANSFIGURATION

> *"(Jesus) took Peter, John and James with him and went up onto a mountain to pray. As he was praying, the appearance of his face changed, and his clothes became as bright as a flash of lightning. Two men, Moses and Elijah, appeared in glorious splendor, talking with Jesus. They spoke about his departure, which he was about to bring to fulfillment at Jerusalem. Peter and his companions were very sleepy, but when they became fully awake, they saw his glory and the two men standing with him. As the men were leaving Jesus, Peter said to him, 'Master, it is good for us to be here. Let us put up three shelters—one for you, one for Moses and one for Elijah.' (though) he did not know what he was saying. While he was speaking, a cloud*

> *appeared and covered them, and they were afraid as they entered the cloud. A voice came from the cloud, saying, 'This is my Son, whom I have chosen; listen to him.' When the voice had spoken, they found that Jesus was alone. The disciples kept this to themselves and did not tell anyone at that time what they had seen." Luke 9:28-36 NIV*

This biblical account we have just read is known as the Transfiguration. Peter suggested that they build three shelters for them, though the scripture says Peter didn't realize fully what he was saying. Peter was seeing a revelation of the corporate church being built. Moses, an Old Testament Apostle, Elijah, an Old Testament Prophet, and Jesus, the Son, our Savior and Chief Cornerstone. Peter was seeing **the pattern**.

> *"Now, therefore, you are no longer strangers and foreigners, but fellow citizens with the saints and members of the household of God, having been built on the foundation of the apostles and prophets, Jesus Christ Himself being the chief cornerstone, in whom the whole building, being fitted together, grows into a holy temple in the*

> *Lord, in whom you also are being built together for a dwelling place of God in the Spirit." Ephesians 2:19-22 NKJV*

Though Peter didn't realize it, there at the Transfiguration was the fulfillment of this scripture, with the presence of the "apostle and prophet" along with the "Chief Cornerstone, Jesus, "*in whom the whole building...grows into a holy temple...in whom you also are being built together...*" Peter saw the components of the glorious church because Christ was revealed in His glory. The Glory manifested in Jesus wasn't His deity as tradition tells us, because He was here as a "Man in the Image of God", the Last Adam! That was the glory that you and I also carry ... the same glory. The glory that was in Him is now in us! The potential glory of the church.

> *"that they all may be one, as You, Father, are in Me, and I in You; that they also may be one in Us, that the world may believe that You sent Me. 22 And the glory which You gave Me I have given them, that they may be one just as We are one: 23 I in them, and You in Me; that they may be made perfect in one, and that the world may know that You have sent Me, and*

> *have loved them as You have loved Me." John 17:21-23 NKJV*

The Glory manifested in Jesus on that day was the "glory of a son." Now we are all "sons of God" and God is "bringing many sons to Glory."

> *"While he was still speaking, behold, a bright cloud overshadowed them; and suddenly a voice came out of the cloud, saying, "This is My beloved Son, in whom I am well pleased. Hear Him!" Matthew 17:5 NKJV*

> *"For it was fitting for Him, for whom are all things and by whom are all things, in bringing many sons to glory, to make the captain of their salvation perfect through sufferings." Hebrews 2:10 NKJV*

We are transformed from "one degree of glory to another" as we "see ourselves in the mirror of God's Word." There we see ourselves as being "in the image of God" again. We must go into the Epistles of Paul and meditate on the New Creation Realities he explained until our mind is renewed and we can see ourselves as God sees us now.

"But we all, with unveiled face, beholding as in a mirror the glory of the Lord, are being transformed into the same image from glory to glory, just as by the Spirit of the Lord." 2 Corinthians 3:18 NKJV

"Behold what manner of love the Father has bestowed on us, that we should be called children of God! Therefore the world does not know us, because it did not know Him. Beloved, now we are children of God; and it has not yet been revealed what we shall be, but we know that when He is revealed, we shall be like Him, for we shall see Him as He is. And everyone who has this hope in Him purifies himself, just as He is pure." 1 John 3:1-3 NKJV

WALKING IN THE REALM OF THE MIRACULOUS

Miracles happened because Jesus walked in that great dimension of the Glory of God. As we progress, miracles, signs, and wonders like we've never seen before will begin to happen in and through us; that's what's going to happen in the Glory of God. (Mark 16:17, 16:20; Acts 2:22, 2:43, 4:16, 4:30, 5:12, 6:8, 8:6,

8:13, 14:3, 15:12; Romans 15:18-19, 1 Corinthians 14:22, 2 Corinthians 12:12, Hebrews 2:4).

> *"This beginning of signs Jesus did in Cana of Galilee, and* ***manifested His glory****; and His disciples believed in Him." John 2:11 NKJV*

> *"Jesus said to her, "Did I not say to you that if you would believe you would* ***see the glory of God?"*** *John 11:40 NKJV*

THE FINAL MANIFESTATION OF GLORY WHEN OUR BODIES ARE CHANGED

> *"Now this I say, brethren, that flesh and blood cannot inherit the kingdom of God; nor does corruption inherit incorruption. Behold, I tell you a mystery: We shall not all sleep, but we shall all be changed— in a moment, in the twinkling of an eye, at the last trumpet. For the trumpet will sound, and the dead will be raised incorruptible, and we shall be changed. For this corruptible must put on incorruption, and this mortal must put on immortality. So when this corruptible has put on incorruption, and this mortal has put*

> *on immortality, then shall be brought to pass the saying that is written: 'Death is swallowed up in victory.' 'O Death, where is your sting?' 'O Hades, where is your victory?' The sting of death is sin, and the strength of sin is the law. But thanks be to God, who gives us the victory through our Lord Jesus Christ. Therefore, my beloved brethren, be steadfast, immovable, always abounding in the work of the Lord, knowing that your labor is not in vain in the Lord." 1 Corinthians 15:50-58 NASB*

This one is the final miracle that we're going to experience. In this scripture, the word "moment" (in the twinkling of an eye) is the Greek word "atomos" which means the smallest division or portion of time. It couldn't be any faster. We're not even going to know it happened. Suddenly, we're just going to start feeling really good! The last miracle we'll need is for our mortality to be changed to immortal; the corruptible to be made incorruptible.

> *"But if the Spirit of Him who raised Jesus from the dead dwells in you, He who raised Christ from the dead will also give life to*

> *your mortal bodies through His Spirit who dwells in you." Romans 8:11 NKJV*

The glory that's in you, the miracle of changing your mortal body into an immortal spiritual body, it's already waiting in you and will happen at the return of Jesus in His Glorified Body.

> *"For our citizenship is in heaven, from which we also eagerly wait for the Savior, the Lord Jesus Christ, 21 who will transform our lowly body that it may be conformed to His glorious body, according to the working by which He is able even to subdue all things to Himself." Philippians 3:20-21 NKJV*

If we can just learn what the Word of God is showing us ... to live according to the pattern, both corporately and individually ... we will develop with each level of growth and maturity and our life will produce another measure of the Glory of God until we walk in that same measure of the glory that Christ walked in. That's God's goal! That's the vision, always with unveiled face, beholding us in the mirror of the Glory of the Lord. We see the potential. We're transformed from one degree of glory to another. The best is yet to come!

CLOSING PRAYER

Father God, I pray for the spirit of wisdom and revelation to be upon us, just as Paul prayed,

> *"that the God of our Lord Jesus Christ, the Father of Glory, may give to us the spirit of wisdom and revelation in the knowledge of Him, the eyes of your understanding being enlightened, that you may know what is the hope of His calling, what are the riches of the Glory of His inheritance in the saints, and what is the exceeding greatness of His power toward us who believe, according to the working of His mighty power." Ephesians 1:17-19 NKJV*

Lord, may we understand how rich we are, and the riches we have is the very Glory of God that increases and increases and increases in our life until one day, when Jesus returns and the trumpet sounds, we get the final miracle from the Glory of God. Father, bring us into the pattern corporately. Give us all revelation of the pattern. As individual Christians, give us revelation of the pattern of the son, Jesus Christ, that you are growing us into His image. We thank you for these things. Lord, You said if we ask anything according to Your will, You hear us. If we know You hear us, we know that we have the petition that we've asked from You (1 John 5:14-15). Lord, we thank You that we have it, the revelation knowledge of Your glory. In Jesus' name, Amen!

About The Author

John Polis was saved and filled with Holy Spirit in 1974 during the Jesus Movement. He attended Dayton Bible College and graduated with a B.A. in Biblical Studies in 1980, after which he became pastor of a Pentecostal church in West Virginia.

In 1983, John had an encounter that transitioned him into the ministry of Apostle. Afterwards, he began to travel as an Evangelist and International Bible Teacher.

Among the works established was Eldoret Bible College in Kenya, Africa, which was birthed in 1998 and has graduated over 2500 students with undergraduate and graduate degrees. Students have planted more than 600 churches throughout Africa to date, some of which have more than 5000 in attendance. John has been a television and radio host for more than 40 years, has authored 30 publications, and has books translated into 7 languages. As President and Founder of Revival Fellowship International, John, and his wife Rebecca, have many spiritual sons and daughters in 13 states and 5 countries. John carries and imparts an Elijah Anointing to prepare the Church for discipling nations as mature sons and daughters. John serves on the Council of Elders for the International Coalition of Apostolic Leaders and is a former United States Marine, being a veteran of the Vietnam War. John and Rebecca have been married 47 years, with 4 children and 9 grandchildren.

BOOKS BY JOHN POLIS

Pattern For Glory: Living In The Manifest Presence Of God.

9 Apostolic Functions: Things Apostles Do.

HardStop: Why You Can't Wait Any Longer To Stop What's Stopping You.

Heartbeat Of An Apostle: Revelation From The Heart Of Paul.

Apostolic Functions: 9 Things Apostles Do.

Built Strong: 31 Keys To Spiritual Power.

God Fathers: How You Can Be One.

Stronger Than Satan: Understanding Your Authority In Christ.

Victorious: How To Face, Fight, and Finish Your Battles.

Release The River Within You: Increasing The Anointing Flow

Put On Your Gloves: The Five Battles Every Christian Must Win

Apostolic Advice: Proven Wisdom for Building Strong Foundations in the Local Church.

Recycled Believers: Solving The Mystery of Migrating Sheep.

How To Produce Abundance In Your Life: The Kingdom Secrets Jesus Taught His Disciples.

Biblical Headship: Making Sense of Submission To Authority.

The Master Builder: Wisdom for Today's Apostles

Take My Yoke Upon You: Fulfilling Your 3 Dimensional Destiny

The Kings Are Coming: Understanding The Kingly Anointing

Renewing The Mind: A Self Study Guide To New Creation Realities

BE STRONG IN THE LORD:
DISCIPLESHIP SERIES BOOKS BY JOHN POLIS

Living Unshakeable In A Shaking World: 6 Principles For Successful Kingdom Living.

Total Victory Is For You: 5 Smooth Stones To Slay Your Giants.

The Love Of God

How To Obtain Strong Faith

Spiritual Warfare: No Place For Satan

For these and additional resources to help you in your spiritual growth, go to www.johnpolis.com.

www.ingramcontent.com/pod-product-compliance
Lightning Source LLC
Chambersburg PA
CBHW060337050426
42449CB00011B/2784
* 9 7 8 1 7 3 7 7 2 3 6 8 4 *